dinosaurs

By Penelope Arlon
and Tory Gordon-Harris

How to discover more

Dinosaurs is packed with prehistoric creatures and filled with great facts about them. By knowing a little bit about the way the book works, you will have fun reading, and discover more.

Dino adventure

The book travels through time to introduce the great dinosaurs of the Triassic, Jurassic, and Cretaceous periods. Learn about fossils, fossil hunters, and amazing dinosaur record setters along the way.

The introduction sets up the big fight scene.

The caption tells you about Stegosaurus' opponent, Allosaurus.

The fact box tells what each dinosaur ate, shows how HUGE it was, and lots more.

NAME MEANING:
"Other lizard"

DIET: Meat

PERIOD:
Jurassic

Stegosaurus vs

Stegosaurus was a giant plant-eating dinosaur with huge plates across its back. It was pretty big, but it still had to watch out for *Allosaurus*!

Tough skin protected Stegosaurus from sharp teeth.

The fight
If *Allosaurus* managed to kill *Stegosaurus*, it had enough to eat for weeks. Let's find out how they might have fought.

STEGOSAURUS
(STEG-oh-SORE-us)

NAME MEANING:
"Roof-lizard"

DIET: Plants

ALLOSAURUS
(AL-oh-SORE-us)

NAME MEANING:
"Other lizard"

DIET: Meat

PERIOD:
Jurassic

Stegosaurus

Huge, thick legs to support a heavy body made Stegosaurus slow.

42   Result: Physically they were evenly matched, but

Digital companion book

Download your free all-new digital book,
Dinosaur Face-Offs

**Log on to
www.scholastic.com/discovermore**

**Enter your unique code:
RCN4MM3P6K3D**

Watch six fierce dinosaur fights

Small words describe the action and give bite-size facts.

The timeline across the top shows when the dinosaurs lived.

Look up a favourite subject in the contents.

Allosaurus

TRIASSIC | JURASSIC | CRETACEOUS

Bony plates kept Allosaurus from leaping onto its back.

Aggressive swipes from Stegosaurus' spiky tail punctured Allosaurus and knocked it to the ground.

The jaws opened incredibly wide and slashed with dozens of small, sharp teeth.

Long, agile back legs made Allosaurus a fast runner.

The labels tell you which dinosaur is which.

Learn how to say dinosaurs' names, and look up or learn new words in the glossary.

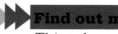
Allosaurus

The hooked claws could grasp, grip, and tear into flesh.

The forearms could grip Stegosaurus' neck so that Allosaurus could bite its throat.

▶▶▶ **Find out more**
about *Velociraptor* vs *Protoceratops* on pages 56–57

Find out more
This takes you to another page to learn about other related facts.

Allosaurus had a bigger brain, so it used its wits to win.

43

The words along the bottom are questions or amazing facts.

Look up a word in the index and find which page it's on.

Teeth

Click the pop-ups for facts and stats

Cretaceous

Encyclopedia entries to discover even more

Guess the silhouettes

Fun dinosaur quizzes

Consultant: Kim Dennis-Bryan, PhD
Art Director: Bryn Walls
Assistant Designers: Clare Joyce, Ali Scrivens
Managing Editor: Miranda Smith

Cover Designers: Neal Cobourne,
Natalie Godwin
DTP: Sunita Gahir
Visual Content Editor: Diane Allford-Trotman
**Executive Director of Photography,
Scholastic:** Steve Diamond

Library of Congress Cataloging-in-Publication
Data Available

Distributed in the UK by
Scholastic UK Ltd
Westfield Road
Southam, Warwickshire
England CV47 0RA

ISBN 978 1407 13464 2

10 9 8 7 6 5 4 3 2 1   12 13 14 15 16

Printed in Singapore   46
First edition, September 2012

Scholastic is constantly working to lessen the
environmental impact of our manufacturing
processes. To view our industry-leading
paper procurement policy, visit
www.scholastic.com/paperpolicy.

Contents

The world of the dinosaurs

For 165 million years, Earth belonged to the dinosaurs. Through thick forests and damp swamps, giant meat-eaters like this *T. rex* bellowed and gnashed their ferocious teeth, looking for prey.

What is a dinosaur?

Dinosaurs were animals that lived millions of years ago. Some were the most colossal creatures ever to have lived on land.

Camarasaurus, one of the biggest dinosaurs, could grow to be 8.5 m (28 ft) long.

Dinosaur skin was scaly, like reptile skin, but some dinosaurs had feathers, too.

Camarasaurus

Standing tall

Dinosaurs had upright stances for faster movement. Other reptiles have slower, sprawling gaits, with their limbs out to the sides.

Camarasaurus *was a giant plant-eater.*

There were no dinosaurs in the ocean, and only a few

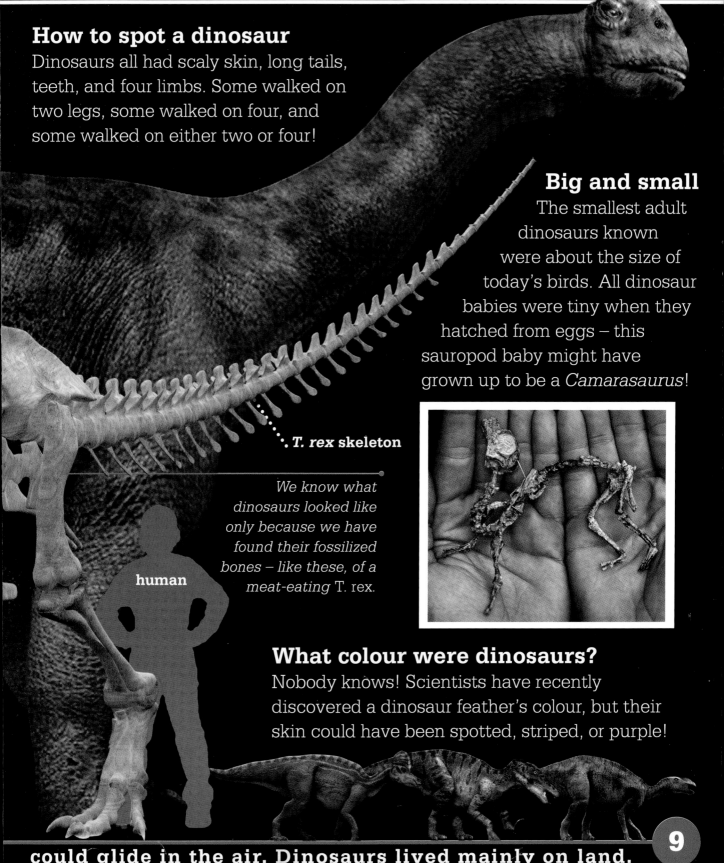

How to spot a dinosaur

Dinosaurs all had scaly skin, long tails, teeth, and four limbs. Some walked on two legs, some walked on four, and some walked on either two or four!

Big and small

The smallest adult dinosaurs known were about the size of today's birds. All dinosaur babies were tiny when they hatched from eggs – this sauropod baby might have grown up to be a *Camarasaurus*!

***T. rex* skeleton**

We know what dinosaurs looked like only because we have found their fossilized bones – like these, of a meat-eating T. rex.

human

What colour were dinosaurs?

Nobody knows! Scientists have recently discovered a dinosaur feather's colour, but their skin could have been spotted, striped, or purple!

could glide in the air. Dinosaurs lived mainly on land.

Hall of fame

Dinosaurs were among the most awe-inspiring animals to have lived on Earth, so the record setters of the dinosaur world were truly amazing!

BIGGEST MEAT-EATER
Giganotosaurus *was one of the biggest meat-eating dinosaurs. It probably hunted Argentinosaurus – what an impressive sight that would have been!*

FASTEST RUNNER
Ostrich-like Gallimimus could probably run at a rate of 65 kph (40 mph) – about as fast as a racehorse.

BIGGEST SKULL
Torosaurus *had a huge skull that stretched 2.6 m (8.5 ft) in length.*

FIRST IN SPACE
In 1985, pieces of Maiasaura bone and eggshell flew into space on a space shuttle.

BIGGEST DINOSAUR
Argentinosaurus *grew up to 35 m (115 ft) in length. That's as long as five African elephants standing trunk to tail!*

MOST TEETH
Some of the plant-eating hadrosaurs had up to 1,000 cheek teeth for grinding food in the sides of their jaws.

WEIRDEST-LOOKING
Therizinosaurus *was a bizarre plant-eating dinosaur with massive claws on the ends of its long arms.*

SMARTEST DINO
Deinonychus *was a speedy, wily dinosaur with a large brain for its body size.*

SMALLEST DINO
Microraptor *was one of the smallest dinosaurs. It was the size of a pigeon.*

BEST ARMOUR
Ankylosaurus *had super-tough plated skin covered with spikes, and a clubbed tail.*

. . . had the longest name.

Life on Earth

Dinosaurs lived between 230 and 65 million years ago. That's a LONG time ago. Life on Earth is divided into periods of time called eras. This is what was living in the eras before and after the dinosaurs.

Precambrian era

Life first appeared on Earth, in the form of tiny living things in water.

Paleozoic era

During this era, the first land animals appeared: insects, reptiles, and cynodonts (early mammal-like animals).

About 350 million years ago, fish with lungs and four limbs first crawled ashore. Life on land began.

· · · · tetrapod

By the late Paleozoic era, huge reptiles, such as Dimetrodon, lived on Earth.

Dimetrodon

· · · dragonfly

Time of mass extinction   Lots of creatures died out.

Mesozoic era

The dinosaurs appeared during this era. It is divided into three periods: Triassic, Jurassic, and Cretaceous.

Triassic · · · ·
Coelophysis

TRIASSIC

MESOZOIC
251–65 MILLION YEARS AGO

Mesozoic periods

TRIASSIC: 251–199 MYA

JURASSIC: 199–145 MYA

CRETACEOUS: 145–65 MYA

(*MYA* stands for "million years ago".)

......Cretaceous *Velociraptor*

JURASSIC

CRETACEOUS

......*Jurassic Allosaurus*

Extinction Many dinosaurs and other creatures died out.

CENOZOIC
65 MILLION YEARS AGO TO PRESENT DAY

Cenozoic era

After the dinosaurs became extinct, or disappeared, mammals grew bigger and became the biggest animals on land.

......human

......*Smilodon*

......mammoth

About 200,000 years ago, Homo sapiens first appeared on Earth.

PRESENT DAY

Mammoths were around until 5,000 years ago.

13

Twelve dinosaurs are shown on the next four pages, from early dinosaurs to the last ones that lived on Earth. Their fossilized remains show us that they existed in all shapes and sizes.

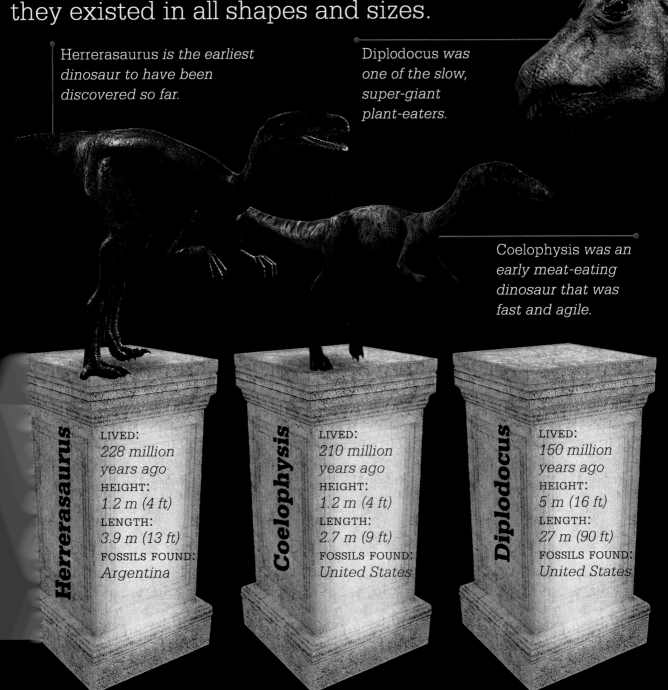

Herrerasaurus *is the earliest dinosaur to have been discovered so far.*

Diplodocus *was one of the slow, super-giant plant-eaters.*

Coelophysis *was an early meat-eating dinosaur that was fast and agile.*

Herrerasaurus

LIVED:
228 million years ago
HEIGHT:
1.2 m (4 ft)
LENGTH:
3.9 m (13 ft)
FOSSILS FOUND:
Argentina

Coelophysis

LIVED:
210 million years ago
HEIGHT:
1.2 m (4 ft)
LENGTH:
2.7 m (9 ft)
FOSSILS FOUND:
United States

Diplodocus

LIVED:
150 million years ago
HEIGHT:
5 m (16 ft)
LENGTH:
27 m (90 ft)
FOSSILS FOUND:
United States

Find out what these dinosaurs ate, how they lived, and

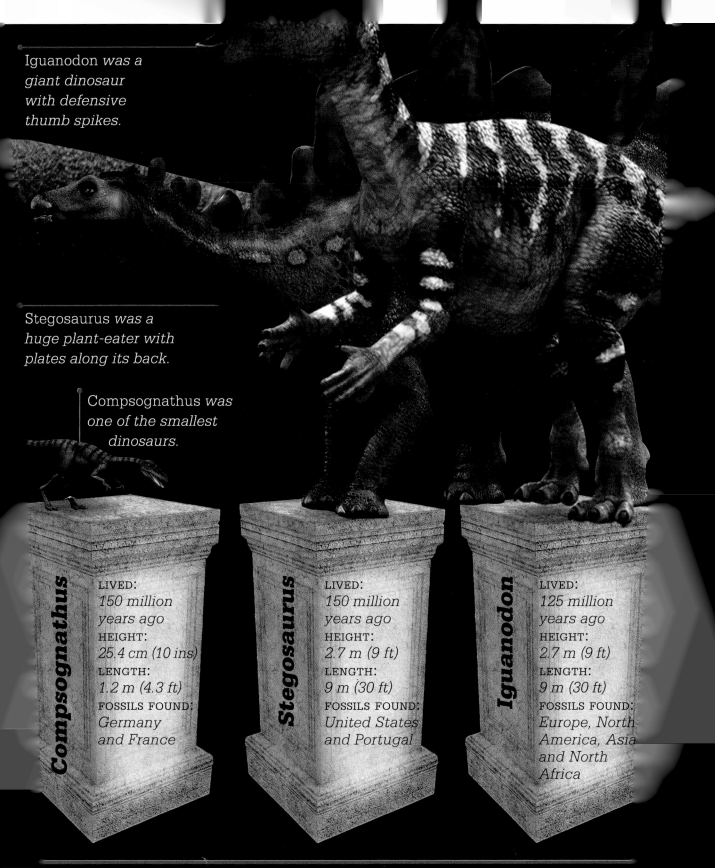

Iguanodon *was a giant dinosaur with defensive thumb spikes.*

Stegosaurus *was a huge plant-eater with plates along its back.*

Compsognathus *was one of the smallest dinosaurs.*

Compsognathus

LIVED:
150 million years ago
HEIGHT:
25.4 cm (10 ins)
LENGTH:
1.2 m (4.3 ft)
FOSSILS FOUND:
Germany and France

Stegosaurus

LIVED:
150 million years ago
HEIGHT:
2.7 m (9 ft)
LENGTH:
9 m (30 ft)
FOSSILS FOUND:
United States and Portugal

Iguanodon

LIVED:
125 million years ago
HEIGHT:
2.7 m (9 ft)
LENGTH:
9 m (30 ft)
FOSSILS FOUND:
Europe, North America, Asia and North Africa

at they might have fought throughout this book.

As time passed, dinosaurs changed body shapes and found new ways to defend themselves. By 65 million years ago, dinosaurs were in their prime.

Spinosaurus *was a massive fish-eating dinosaur with a huge sail on its back.*

Edmontosaurus *probably lived in large herds for safety.*

Velociraptor *was a feathered dinosaur tha... hunted in packs.*

Spinosaurus

LIVED:
99–93 million years ago
HEIGHT:
6.1 m (20 ft)
LENGTH:
15.8 m (52 ft)
FOSSILS FOUND:
Egypt and Morocco

Edmontosaurus

LIVED:
75 million years ago
HEIGHT:
2.7 m (9 ft)
LENGTH:
12.8 m (42 ft)
FOSSILS FOUND:
Canada and United States

Velociraptor

LIVED:
75–71 million years ago
HEIGHT:
1 m (3 ft)
LENGTH:
1.8 m (6 ft)
FOSSILS FOUND:
Mongolia, Russia, and China

We know of about 540 kinds of dinosaur, but as ma...

Tyrannosaurus rex *had bigger teeth than any other dinosaur yet discovered.*

Ankylosaurus *had a very well-armoured body and a clubbed tail to protect itself.*

Triceratops *had huge horns and a giant frill.*

Ankylosaurus

LIVED:
70–65 million years ago
HEIGHT:
1.2 m (4 ft)
LENGTH:
10 m (33 ft)
FOSSILS FOUND:
Canada and United States

Tyrannosaurus rex

LIVED:
70–65 million years ago
HEIGHT:
6.1 m (20 ft)
LENGTH:
12.4 m (40 ft)
FOSSILS FOUND:
United States and Mongolia

Triceratops

LIVED:
70–65 million years ago
HEIGHT:
2.1 m (7 ft)
LENGTH:
9 m (30 ft)
FOSSILS FOUND:
Canada and United States

900 kinds might have lived, or perhaps more

Dinosaur detectives

Nobody has seen a dinosaur alive – we can only study their fossilized remains. But with a little detective work, fossil experts called paleontologists can find out what dinosaurs looked like, and sometimes how they behaved.

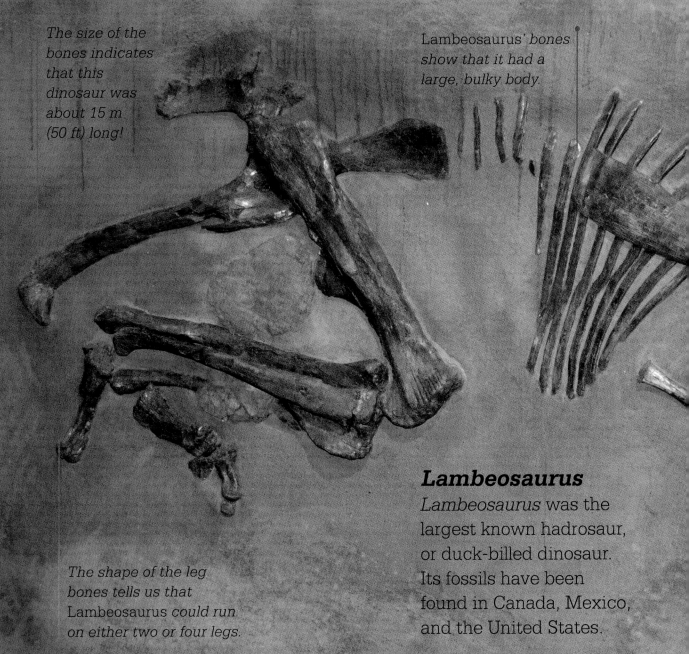

The size of the bones indicates that this dinosaur was about 15 m (50 ft) long!

Lambeosaurus' bones show that it had a large, bulky body.

The shape of the leg bones tells us that Lambeosaurus *could run on either two or four legs.*

Lambeosaurus

Lambeosaurus was the largest known hadrosaur, or duck-billed dinosaur. Its fossils have been found in Canada, Mexico, and the United States.

Studies of the rocks around the *Lambeosaurus* fossils

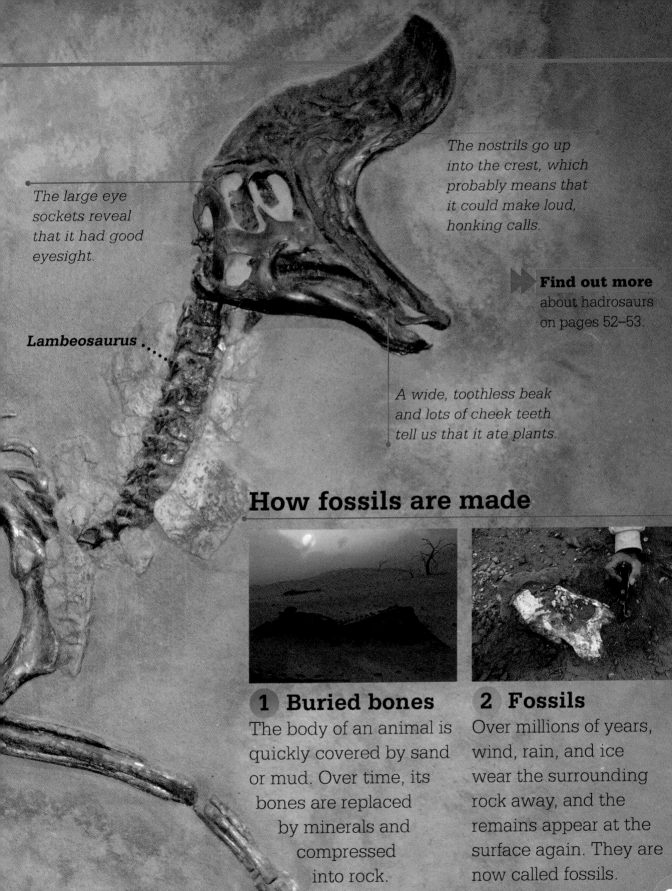

The large eye sockets reveal that it had good eyesight.

The nostrils go up into the crest, which probably means that it could make loud, honking calls.

Find out more about hadrosaurs on pages 52–53.

Lambeosaurus

A wide, toothless beak and lots of cheek teeth tell us that it ate plants.

How fossils are made

1 Buried bones
The body of an animal is quickly covered by sand or mud. Over time, its bones are replaced by minerals and compressed into rock.

2 Fossils
Over millions of years, wind, rain, and ice wear the surrounding rock away, and the remains appear at the surface again. They are now called fossils.

show that the dinosaur lived in the Cretaceous period.

Fossil clues

Bones
Fossilized bones tell us what a dinosaur looked like, and the surrounding rocks give clues to help paleontologists work out how long ago the dinosaur lived.

Footprints
The tracks and strides shown in fossilized footprints tell scientists how fast an animal ran, how heavy it was, and if it moved in a group.

Skin
Only a few examples of dinosaur skin or skin impressions have been found. However, from these fossils, we know that dinosaurs had scaly skin.

Feathers
A few fossils have shown that some dinosaurs had feathers on their bodies.

The feathers were very similar to these bird feathers.

New fossil evidence is being found all the time. And

Coprolites

A coprolite is fossilized animal poo. Dinosaur coprolites can tell us about the dinosaur's last meal. Dinosaur poo may contain seeds, wood, leaves, fish, or bones.

Eggs

Fossils prove that dinosaurs laid eggs. Scientists have found fossilized eggs with adult dinosaur fossils, which means that some dinosaur parents looked after their eggs.

Plants

Fossilized plants found near dinosaur bones give us clues about what plants were growing at the time and therefore what particular dinosaurs may have eaten.

Animals today

Scientists study animals today to try to explain how dinosaurs might have behaved. This African wild dog hunts in packs, perhaps like many dinosaurs did.

there is so much more out there to discover!

Dinosaur guesswork

Often only small parts of a dinosaur are discovered, so paleontologists have to work out what the whole dino looked like. There's a lot they disagree on, and much more to find out!

Lonely skull

Only the skull of *Pachycephalosaurus* has been found. It has an unusual hard dome on the top.

Some paleontologists think that males butted one another to fight over females.

Picturing a dinosaur

After comparing *Pachycephalosaurus'* skull with skulls of different dinosaurs, scientists think that it may have had a bulky body, walked on two legs, and used a heavy tail to help it balance.

Pachycephalosaurus skull

Pachycephalosaurus illustration, based on the skull and on other dinosaurs

Iguanodon mystery

When Gideon Mantell dug up *Iguanodon* bones in 1825, the study of dinosaurs was new, so his ideas had mistakes. But in 1834, a more complete *Iguanodon* skeleton was found.

Mantell thought Iguanodon *was a mammal-like lizard.*

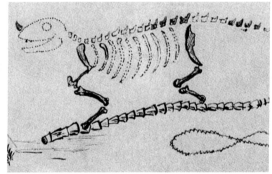

He thought Iguanodon's *spike was on its nose!*

Now we know it was a dinosaur, with a spike on its thumb.

dinosaurs

Triassic and Jurassic

Between 230 and 145 million years ago, during the Triassic and Jurassic periods, giant meat-eaters like *Allosaurus* and massive plant-eaters such as *Stegosaurus* clashed in dramatic fights.

Triassic and Jurassic

The first dinosaurs appeared in the Triassic period. By the end of the Jurassic period, giant meat-eaters and colossal plant-eaters roamed Earth.

Gargoyleosaurus

Mussaurus

Dilophosaurus

Ornitholestes

Archaeopteryx

Herrerasaurus

Dacentrurus

Scelidosaurus

Heterodontosaurus

Allosaurus

Shunosaurus

Compsognathus

Elaphrosaurus

Kentrosaurus

Plateosaurus

Barapasaurus

Dryosaurus

Eoraptor

Monolophosaurus

Apatosaurus

Other ancient creatures

No dinosaurs lived in the ocean. But at the same time that dinosaurs roamed the land, huge meat-eating reptiles lurked beneath the waves, and others flew overhead!

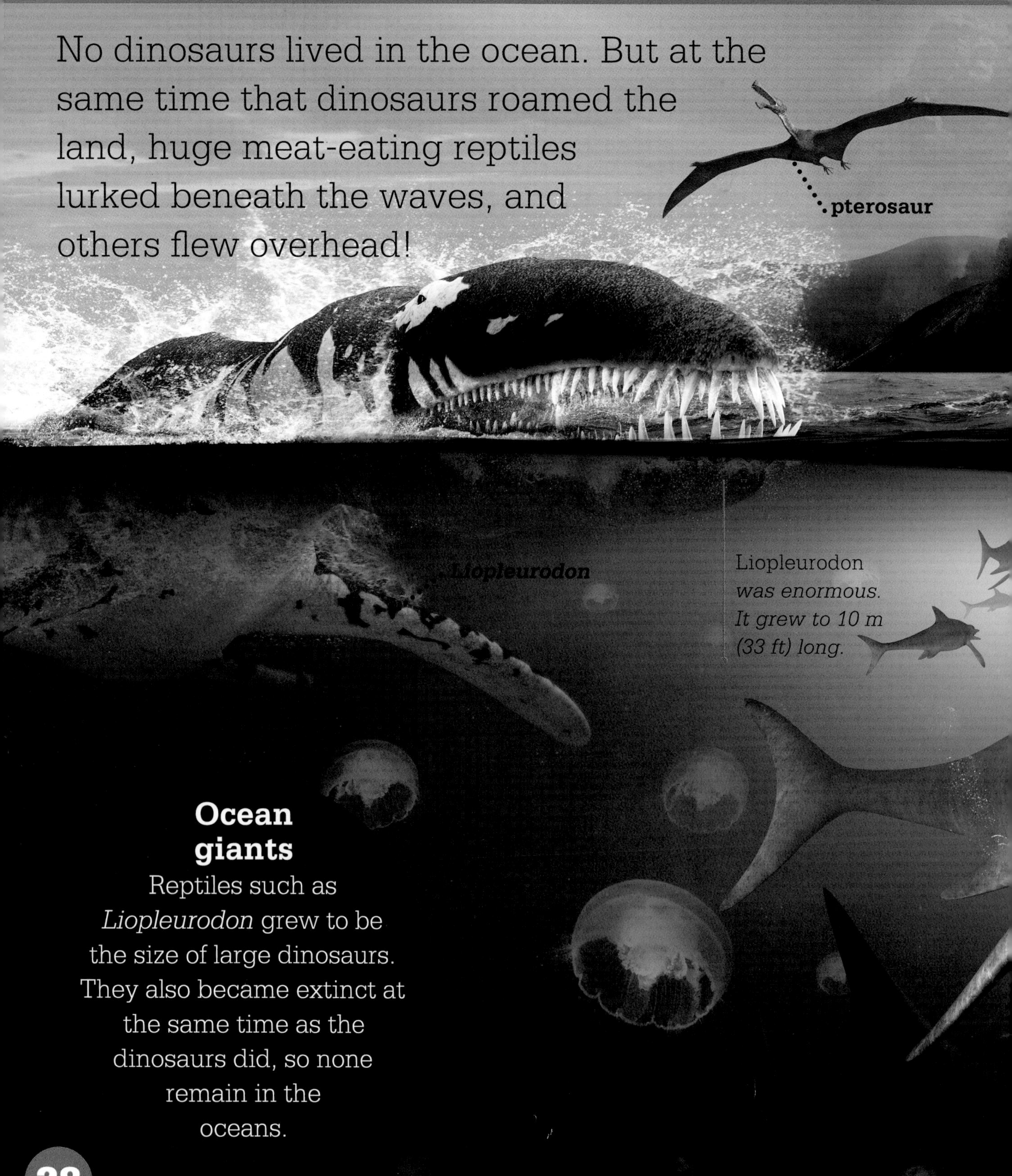

pterosaur

Liopleurodon

Liopleurodon *was enormous. It grew to 10 m (33 ft) long.*

Ocean giants

Reptiles such as *Liopleurodon* grew to be the size of large dinosaurs. They also became extinct at the same time as the dinosaurs did, so none remain in the oceans.

Giant ocean reptiles are long gone, but some fish and

What else lived on land?

Dinosaurs were not the only creatures that lived on land during prehistoric times.

Giant flying reptiles called pterosaurs flew through the skies, some the size of small aeroplanes.

Ichthyosaurs looked like fish but were actually reptiles.

ichthyosaur

Insects like this dragonfly flew around before, during, and after the time of the dinosaurs.

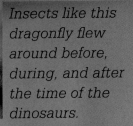

Huge land reptiles hunted the dinosaurs. Some of them were as long as a bus!

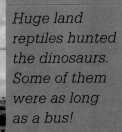

All of the mammals in the dinosaurs' world were small. Many looked like the rats and shrews of today.

Jellyfish and many other creatures haven't changed much since dinosaur days.

Herrerasaurus is the oldest dinosaur to have been found so far. It lived about 228 million years ago. Its fossils were first found in 1956 by a rancher in South America.

Its long, pointy head had small, sharp teeth for gripping prey.

Early meat-eater

Herrerasaurus was one of the biggest dinosaur hunters of its time. It ran on two legs and had a long tail to help it balance.

HERRERASAURUS
(herr-ray-rah-SORE-us)

NAME MEANING:
"Herrera's lizard"

PERIOD:
Triassic

DIET: Meat

Discovery!

Find a brand-new dinosaur, and it might be named after you! Victorino Herrera was the rancher who first spotted *Herrerasaurus* fossils in Argentina.

In 1988, the first intact *Herrerasaurus* skull was found.

Coelophysis

Coelophysis was a fast, vicious meat-eating dinosaur of the Triassic period. It was the size of a small car.

Coelophysis had large eyes, which means it had good eyesight for hunting.

Look out!

Coelophysis was at war with other Triassic reptiles. It could catch smaller ones, but it was hunted by large predators such as phytosaurs, giant crocodile lookalikes that were as long as school buses.

Coelophysis was fast enough to catch small reptiles.

Death in an instant?

Many *Coelophysis* fossils were found together at Ghost Ranch, New Mexico, USA, as if a huge catastrophe, such as a flash flood, killed them all at once.

COELOPHYSIS
(seel-OH-fie-siss)

NAME MEANING:
"Hollow form"

PERIOD:
Triassic

DIET: Meat (small reptiles)

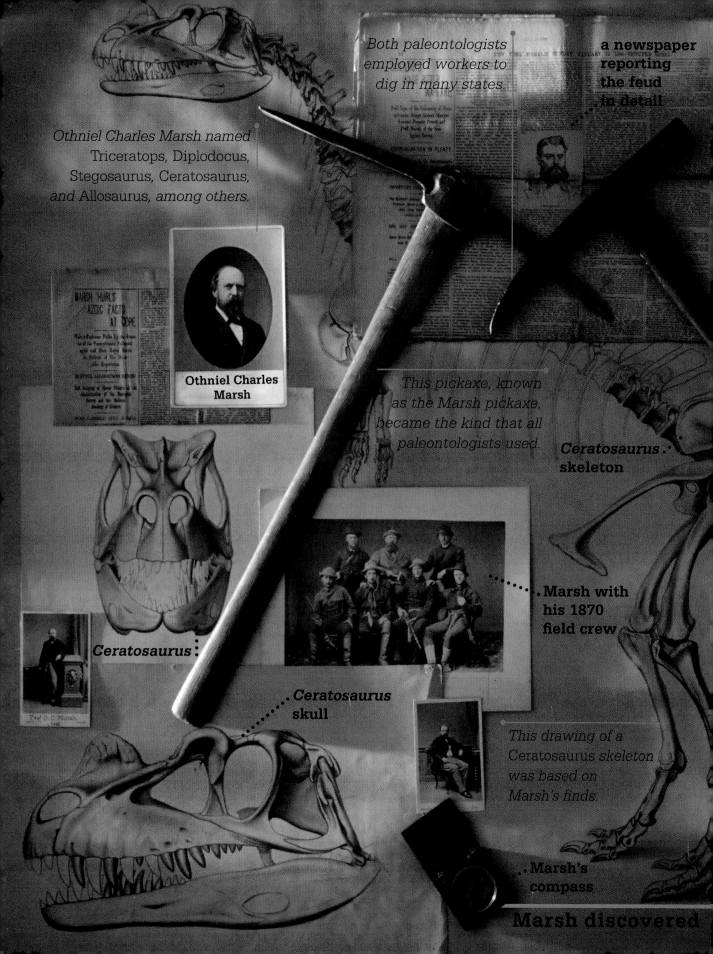

Both paleontologists employed workers to dig in many states.

a newspaper reporting the feud in detail

Othniel Charles Marsh named Triceratops, Diplodocus, Stegosaurus, Ceratosaurus, and Allosaurus, among others.

MARSH HURLS AZOIC FACTS AT COPE

Othniel Charles Marsh

This pickaxe, known as the Marsh pickaxe, became the kind that all paleontologists used.

Ceratosaurus skeleton

Ceratosaurus

Marsh with his 1870 field crew

Ceratosaurus skull

This drawing of a Ceratosaurus skeleton was based on Marsh's finds.

Marsh's compass

Marsh discovered

The Bone Wars

In the late 1800s, a huge number of dinosaurs were found by two American paleontologists, Marsh and Cope, who aggressively competed to discover the most.

Edward Drinker Cope named Coelophysis, Camarasaurus, and giant pterodactyls.

Edward Drinker Cope

dinosaur claw fossil

Cope's skull

some of Cope's artefacts, wrapped in newspapers from the 1890s

Cope's field diary

Dino race

Marsh and Cope bribed people, stole fossils, and even destroyed some to keep the other one from finding them. Once, their teams even threw stones at each other! But they did discover 136 new dinosaurs

80 dinosaurs and Cope discovered 56 – so Marsh won.

Dinosaur eggs

Dinosaurs laid eggs. We know this because egg fossils and nests have been found. Some nests still had fossilized eggs and young in them.

Giant egg
This huge egg, found in China and thought to be from a therizinosaur, is the biggest dinosaur egg ever found.

Maiasaura
Lots of *Maiasaura* nests have been found in Montana, USA. The nests – holes scooped out of the mud – are near one another, indicating that *Maiasaura* lived in groups.

Maiasaura *young found in nests had weak legs, which means that the mother had to feed and care for her babies.*

▶▶ **Find out more** about *Protoceratops* on pages 56–57.

The Montana site where many *Maiasaura*

Oviraptor

This fossil was found in the Gobi Desert, Mongolia. It shows an *Oviraptor* sitting on her nest of eggs. She probably sat on them to keep them warm and safe, just like birds do today.

female *Oviraptor*

egg

Protoceratops

Protoceratops laid its eggs in the hot sands of the Gobi Desert. A fossil *Protoceratops* nest with 12 eggs in it has been found.

Scientists think that dino eggs were leathery and soft – more like reptile eggs than bird eggs.

nests have been found is called Egg Mountain.

Diplodocus

Diplodocus *moved very slowly on all four of its thick legs.*

By the Jurassic period, the giants had appeared. *Diplodocus* was a member of the super-huge sauropod group.

It is thought that Diplodocus *laid its eggs while walking along!*

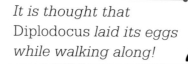

DIPLODOCUS
(DI-plod-oh-kuss)

NAME MEANING:
"Double beam"

PERIOD:
Jurassic

DIET: Plants

Teeth

Diplodocus had small, peg-shaped teeth at the front of its jaws, to tear off leaves. It had no back teeth, so it would have swallowed without chewing.

Diplodocus tooth

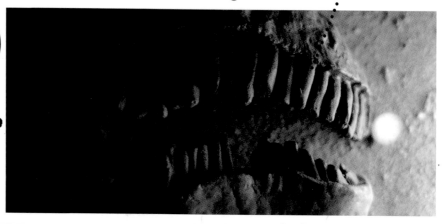

Diplodocus **would have swallowed small stones**

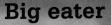
Big eater

Diplodocus had an appetite as large as its body. It probably ate for up to 20 hours a day to maintain its massive body size.

Diplodocus *was about as long as two school buses!*

Diplodocus *had a long tail that it could have used to whip its enemies.*

Find out more about sauropods on the next pages.

Footprints

Fossil footprints of sauropods walking together tell us that they lived in herds. Imagine seeing a herd of *Diplodocus* dinosaurs walking by!

Each footprint is as big as a child's bathtub.

37

to help grind up the unchewed plants in its stomach.

The sauropods were the longest, tallest, and heaviest animals EVER to live on land. They were huge!

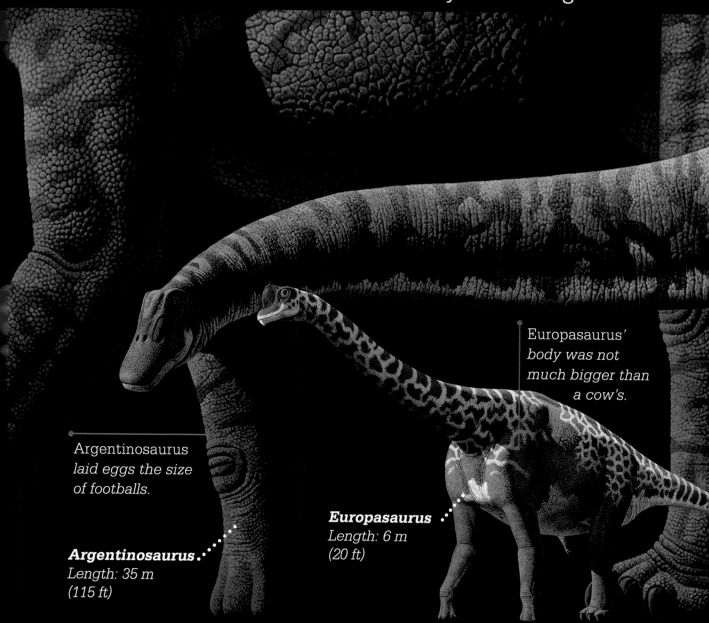

Europasaurus' body was not much bigger than a cow's.

Argentinosaurus laid eggs the size of footballs.

Europasaurus
Length: 6 m
(20 ft)

Argentinosaurus
Length: 35 m
(115 ft)

Argentinosaurus

Argentinosaurus was probably the biggest sauropod, dinosaur, and land animal of all. It was truly colossal – it weighed as much as 14 elephants!

Europasaurus

Bones from *Europasaurus* were thought to be from a baby sauropod until scientists realized they were actually from an adult mini-sauropod.

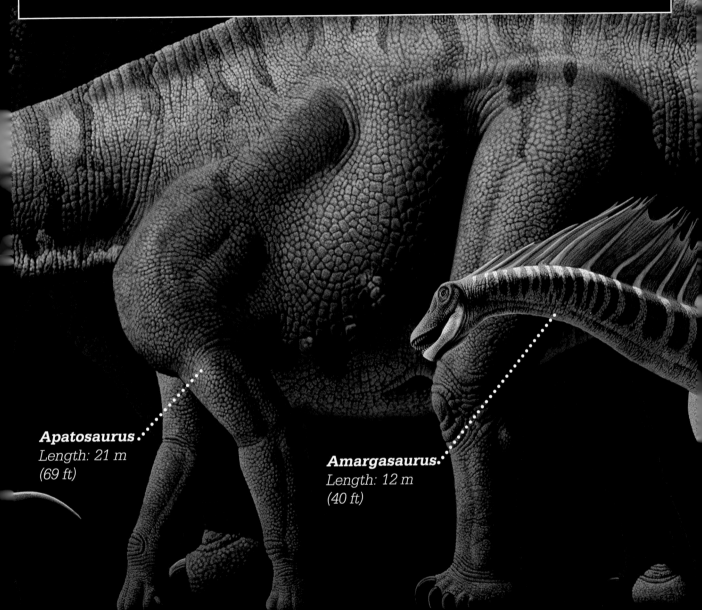

A living super-giant

Sauropods were the biggest land animals, but no creature has ever been as big as the blue whale, which is alive today!

Apatosaurus
*Length: 21 m
(69 ft)*

Amargasaurus
*Length: 12 m
(40 ft)*

Apatosaurus

Apatosaurus was a huge dinosaur. Despite its size, scientists think that it may have been able to rear onto its hind legs to reach leaves.

Amargasaurus

Amargasaurus had two rows of spines growing out of its backbone. They were probably covered in skin and looked a bit like a sail.

Compsognathus

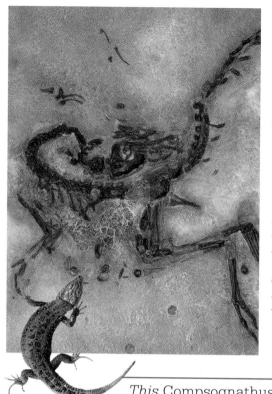

Compsognathus is one of the smallest dinosaurs ever found. It was fast, a meat-eater, and about the size of a turkey.

Lizard lunch

This *Compsognathus* fossil has a lizard in its stomach. The lizard was a fast-moving one, so this dinosaur must have been a quick hunter with good eyesight.

This Compsognathus's last meal was a Bavarisaurus, like this lizard.

A fossil showing part of the skin on Compsognathus' tail suggests that it was scaly.

Compsognathus

Small but deadly

Compsognathus was a fierce little dinosaur with a small head and a mouth filled with sharp, deadly teeth.

Find out more about an even smaller dinosaur on pages 58–59.

Two complete *Compsognathus* skeletons were found in

lion
tooth

Troodon
tooth

human
incisor

Terrible teeth

Meat-eating teeth tend to
be sharp and pointed. Some
are also very, very big!

T. rex
tooth

Megalosaurus
tooth

Compsognathus *could
have had feathers,
but there is no proof.*

Fast and athletic

Compsognathus was built
for speed. It ran on two thin
legs and had a light body, a
long tail for balance when
turning corners quickly, and
a long, flexible neck.

COMPSOGNATHUS
(komp-sog-NATH-us)

NAME MEANING:
"Elegant jaw"

PERIOD:
Jurassic

DIET: Meat

the 1800s,   one in France and one in Germany.

Stegosaurus vs

Stegosaurus was a giant plant-eating dinosaur with huge plates across its back. It was pretty big, but it still had to watch out for *Allosaurus*!

Tough skin protected Stegosaurus from sharp teeth.

The fight

If *Allosaurus* managed to kill *Stegosaurus*, it had enough to eat for weeks. Let's find out how they might have fought.

STEGOSAURUS
(STEG-oh-SORE-us)

NAME MEANING:
"Roof lizard"

DIET: Plants

ALLOSAURUS
(AL-oh-SORE-us)

NAME MEANING:
"Other lizard"

DIET: Meat

PERIOD:
Jurassic

Stegosaurus

Huge, thick legs to support a heavy body made Stegosaurus *slow*.

Result: Physically they were evenly matched, but

Allosaurus

Bony plates kept Allosaurus from leaping onto its back.

The jaws opened incredibly wide and slashed with dozens of small, sharp teeth.

Aggressive swipes from Stegosaurus' spiky tail punctured Allosaurus and knocked it to the ground.

Long, agile back legs made Allosaurus a fast runner.

Allosaurus

The hooked claws could grasp, grip, and tear into flesh.

The forearms could grip Stegosaurus' neck so that Allosaurus could bite its throat.

Find out more
about *Velociraptor* vs *Protoceratops* on pages 56–57.

Allosaurus **had a bigger brain, so it used its wits to win.**

Jurassic rock

If you visit the area, you can still see about 1,500 bones embedded in the rock.

Paleontologists carefully remove the rock to find the

Fossils

This amazing quarry has produced more Jurassic dinosaur fossils – including *Stegosaurus*, *Apatosaurus*, and the giant meat-eater *Allosaurus* – than anywhere else in the world.

fossils. Can you spot any bones around them?

Cretaceous dinosaurs

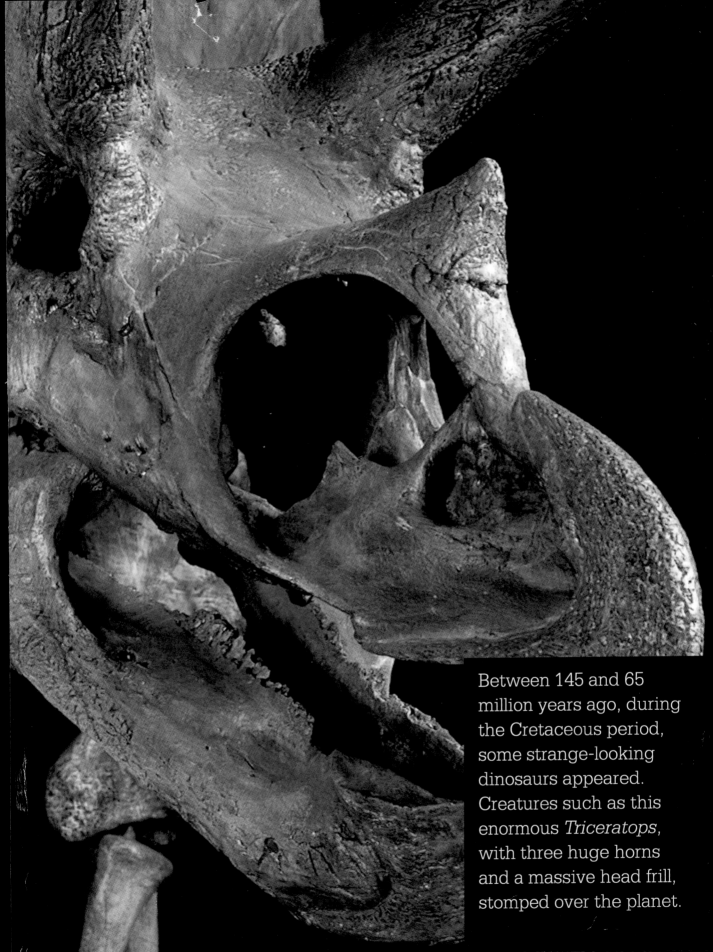

Between 145 and 65 million years ago, during the Cretaceous period, some strange-looking dinosaurs appeared. Creatures such as this enormous *Triceratops*, with three huge horns and a massive head frill, stomped over the planet.

Cretaceous collection

During the Cretaceous period, there was a huge variety of dinosaurs. There were big ones and small ones – some with crests, horns, or spines.

Anatotita

Gryposaurus

Carnotaurus

Hypselosaurus

Amargasaurus

Utahraptor

Troodon

Corythosaurus

Giganotosaurus

Struthiosaurus

Torosaurus

Rhabdodon

Baryonyx

Isisaurus

Gallimimus

Oviraptor

Polacanthus

Edmontonia

Psittacosaurus

Dromaeosaurus

Brachylophosaurus

Ouranosaurus

Mononykus

Iguanodon

Iguanodon was one of the first dinosaurs to be discovered. It was first found in England but has since turned up all over the world.

Iguanodon had strong teeth that ground up tough plants.

Worldwide dinosaur

Iguanodon was once a very common animal on Earth. Its bones have been found in North Africa, Central Asia, and North America, as well as in Europe.

Sharp thumb spikes were used as defensive weapons.

Iguanodon herds

Many *Iguanodon* fossils have been found together, which suggests that they lived in big herds.

IGUANODON
(ig-WAH-noh-don)

NAME MEANING:
"Iguana tooth"

PERIOD:
Cretaceous

DIET: Plants

Iguanodon could run quite fast on two or four legs.

Spinosaurus

Spinosaurus would have been a frightening sight, with its dragon-like sail and super-sharp teeth.

The huge sail stood 2 m (6 ft) above the back. It was supported by bony spines.

Fish-eater

Scientists thought that dinosaurs ate only meat or plants, until they discovered *Spinosaurus* – it was a meat-eater that caught and ate fish, too.

Its nostrils were high up on its nose so that most of its head could reach into water.

Fishing dinosaur

Spinosaurus had sharp claws, and long jaws with knife-edged teeth – both ideal for catching slippery fish.

SPINOSAURUS
(SPINE-oh-SORE-us)

NAME MEANING:
"Spine lizard"

PERIOD:
Cretaceous

DIET: Meat and fish

Spinosaurus was ENORMOUS! It was as big as *T. rex*.

Edmontosaurus

Edmontosaurus was a massive hadrosaur, or duck-billed dinosaur. It was a plant-eater that lived in large herds in swampy areas.

Quick senses

Edmontosaurus was a slow-moving dinosaur, but its skull shows that it may have had good eyesight, hearing, and sense of smell – to keep it alert to large reptiles lurking in the water!

Using the latest technology, scientists have discovered

Hadrosaurs

Hadrosaurs are well known for crests on their skulls. Some may have used their hollow crests for display, or as trumpets that could make loud calls.

Corythosaurus had a large plate-like crest.

Lambeosaurus had a forward-pointing crest.

Parasaurolophus had a long, hollow crest.

Edmontosaurus *may have had loose skin around its nose, which it might have blown out like a balloon as a display or to make calls.*

Edmontosaurus *had a bumpy ridge down its back.*

EDMONTOSAURUS
(ed-MON-toh-SORE-us)

NAME MEANING:
"Lizard of Edmonton (Canada)"

PERIOD:
Cretaceous

DIET: Plants

the bones of up to 10,000 *Edmontosaurus* in one area!

Amazing skulls

Skull fossils of all shapes and sizes tell us what a dinosaur ate, how well it could see, and even how it defended itself.

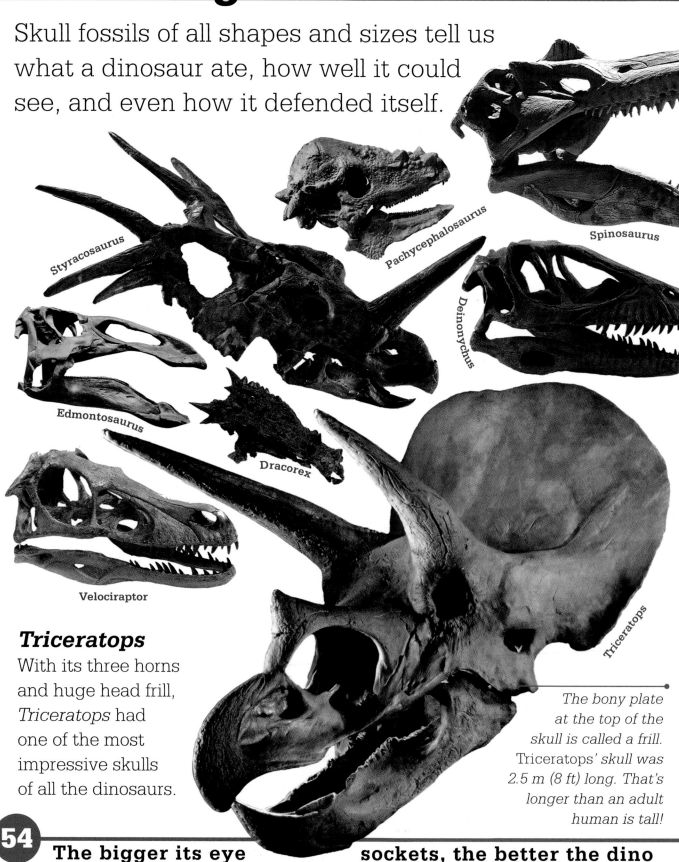

Styracosaurus

Pachycephalosaurus

Spinosaurus

Deinonychus

Edmontosaurus

Dracorex

Velociraptor

Triceratops

With its three horns and huge head frill, *Triceratops* had one of the most impressive skulls of all the dinosaurs.

Triceratops

The bony plate at the top of the skull is called a frill. Triceratops' skull was 2.5 m (8 ft) long. That's longer than an adult human is tall!

The bigger its eye **sockets, the better the dino**

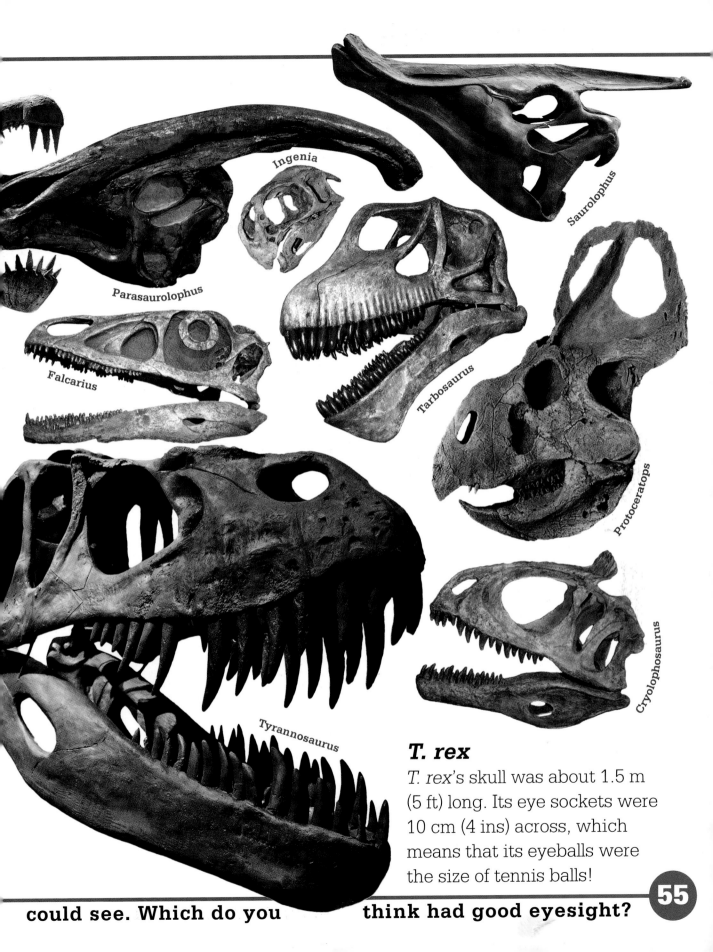

Ingenia

Saurolophus

Parasaurolophus

Falcarius

Tarbosaurus

Protoceratops

Cryolophosaurus

Tyrannosaurus

T. rex

T. rex's skull was about 1.5 m (5 ft) long. Its eye sockets were 10 cm (4 ins) across, which means that its eyeballs were the size of tennis balls!

could see. Which do you · **think had good eyesight?**

Velociraptor VS Protoceratops

Velociraptor was a small but ferocious predator that probably hunted in packs. Survival was tricky for dinosaurs like *Protoceratops* when *Velociraptor* was hungry.

A swipe from the thick tail threw Velociraptor off balance.

Velociraptor

Protoceratops could not keep track of Velociraptor's position in the pack.

VELOCIRAPTOR
(vel-OSS-ee-RAP-tor)

NAME MEANING:
"Quick thief"

DIET: Meat

PROTOCERATOPS
(pro-toe-SERR-ah-tops)

NAME MEANING:
"First horned face"

DIET: Plants

PERIOD:
Cretaceous

The fight

Velociraptor preyed on *Protoceratops*, which was similar in size. Which dinosaur would have won the fight?

Velociraptor was lightly feathered.

Dagger-like claws on the arms and feet gripped Protoceratops while Velociraptor pulled it down.

Result: *Protoceratops* could have wounded *Velociraptor*,

An enlarged claw on each foot slashed into flesh.

Protoceratops

A thick head and a sharp beak gripped and bit Velociraptor.

Tiny, sharp teeth tore into Protoceratops' tough skin.

Velociraptor

Protoceratops

Dino fight

In 1971, a double fossil was found in the Gobi Desert, Mongolia – a *Velociraptor* and a *Protoceratops* locked in battle.

but a lone *Protoceratops* stood no chance against a pack.

Gliding dinosaurs

Microraptor, discovered in China in 2000, is the smallest dinosaur ever found. It had feathers on its arms and legs and is thought to have glided through forests with all of its limbs stretched out.

The diamond-shaped tail would have helped keep the dinosaur stable while gliding.

Nobody knows what colour the feathers were. They could have been brightly coloured.

Dino-birds
Many paleontologists think that *Microraptor* was an ancestor of the modern birds that we know today.

Microraptor *had*
claws on its forewings,
which it probably used
to climb up trees.

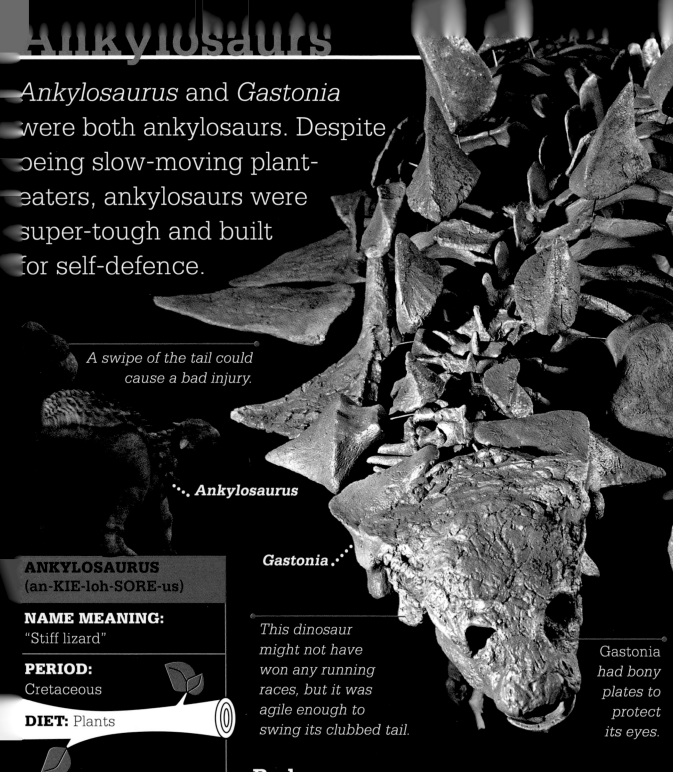

Ankylosaurs

Ankylosaurus and *Gastonia* were both ankylosaurs. Despite being slow-moving plant-eaters, ankylosaurs were super-tough and built for self-defence.

A swipe of the tail could cause a bad injury.

Ankylosaurus

Gastonia

ANKYLOSAURUS
(an-KIE-loh-SORE-us)

NAME MEANING:
"Stiff lizard"

PERIOD:
Cretaceous

DIET: Plants

This dinosaur might not have won any running races, but it was agile enough to swing its clubbed tail.

Gastonia had bony plates to protect its eyes.

Body armour
The best defence an ankylosaur had was its own body. It was a heavy, stocky dinosaur protected by thick bands of bone, which were studded with bony plates or spines.

The only way to injure these super-tough dinosaurs

How to avoid being eaten

Some ankylosaurs may have lived in groups. Other plant-eating dinosaurs, such as *Protoceratops*, also lived in large herds. They defended one another when under attack.

Defensive tails

The tail was a key weapon in a dinosaur fight. A quick lash of the tail might take even the fiercest hunter by surprise or cause an injury.

Ankylosaurus *had a bony, club-like tail that gave fierce blows.*

Kentrosaurus *and* Stegosaurus *had spiky tails that could pierce skin.*

Supersaurus *may have used its tail to swipe at enemies.*

was to flip them over and attack their bellies.

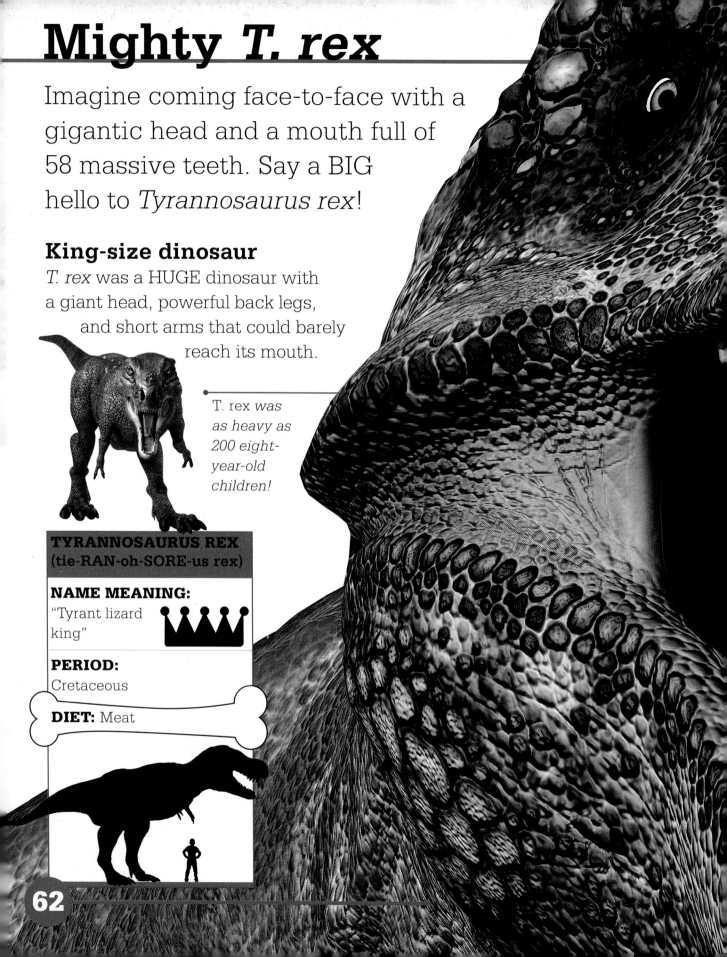

Mighty *T. rex*

Imagine coming face-to-face with a gigantic head and a mouth full of 58 massive teeth. Say a BIG hello to *Tyrannosaurus rex*!

King-size dinosaur

T. rex was a HUGE dinosaur with a giant head, powerful back legs, and short arms that could barely reach its mouth.

T. rex was as heavy as 200 eight-year-old children!

TYRANNOSAURUS REX
(tie-RAN-oh-SORE-us rex)

NAME MEANING:
"Tyrant lizard king"

PERIOD:
Cretaceous

DIET: Meat

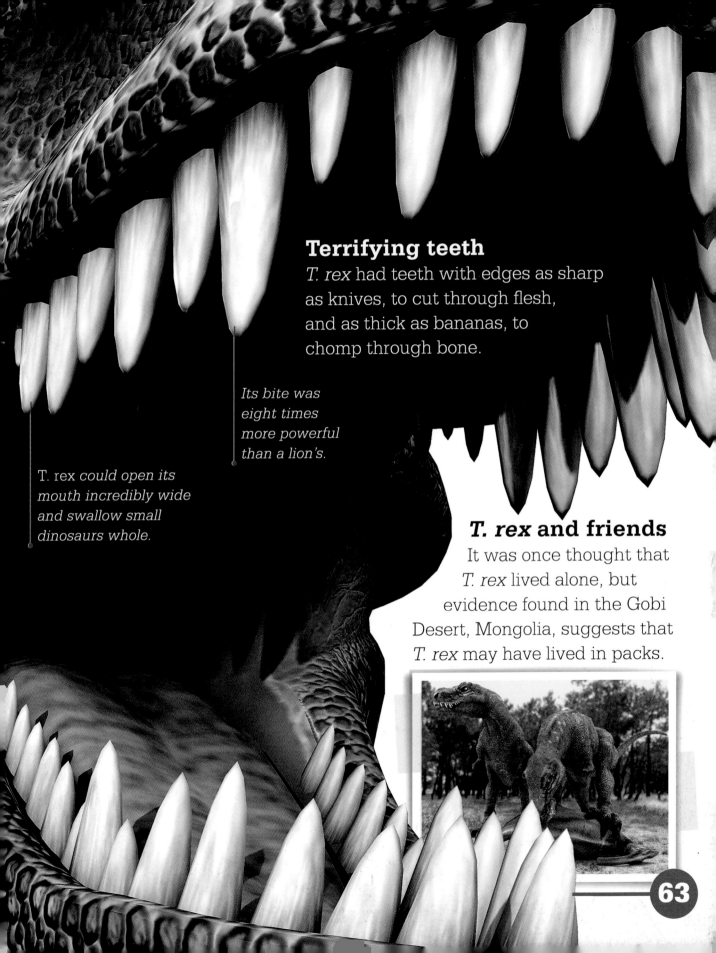

Terrifying teeth

T. rex had teeth with edges as sharp as knives, to cut through flesh, and as thick as bananas, to chomp through bone.

Its bite was eight times more powerful than a lion's.

T. rex could open its mouth incredibly wide and swallow small dinosaurs whole.

T. rex and friends

It was once thought that *T. rex* lived alone, but evidence found in the Gobi Desert, Mongolia, suggests that *T. rex* may have lived in packs.

A GIANT DISCOVERY!

Lucky breakdown

All because of a flat tyre!

In the summer of 1990, Sue Hendrickson was looking for fossils in South Dakota when the team of paleontologists she was with got a flat tyre. While it was being changed, Sue wandered off to check out a rock she had spotted earlier. It turned out to hold the biggest *Tyrannosaurus rex* fossil ever discovered. The dinosaur was named Sue.

Sue lived 67 million

The LARGEST and MOST COMPLETE

Turn over the page to discover how the team dug up Sue and rebuilt the complete skeleton.

Sue Hendrikson and the team with the *T. rex* skull.

A great display

The full skeleton displayed in a museum is actually an exact copy of Sue's bones. Her real bones are too precious to display. They are kept safe so that they don't get broken.

Sue's skull is huge, and so are her teeth. Luckily, she isn't around now to gobble us up!

years ago

TYRANNOSAURUS REX ever discovered

How old is Sue?

Plants were buried and fossilized with Sue, so plant experts looked at them to form an idea about when Sue lived. Geologists (rock experts) also looked at the rocks from which the fossils of the *T. rex* were taken. Together, the scientists worked out that Sue lived about 67 million years ago.

The team used scanners to photograph the bones, then created a digital image of Sue on a computer.

Bone detectives

By looking at Sue's bones, the team found the following facts:

- Sue received several injuries from fights with other dinosaurs – she even had broken bones that had later healed.
- Her bones showed signs of arthritis, a bone disease that humans can develop as they age.

Digging up Sue

Where was Sue?

Sue was discovered in South Dakota, USA, where many fossils have been found. The team also found *Edmontosaurus* fossils there.

Digging out Sue

The team exposed Sue's bones with tiny tools and brushes that removed the rock around them. It took 6 people 17 days to dig out Sue's bones.

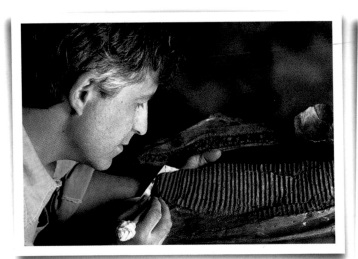

Cleaning Sue

Fossil specialists carefully cleaned the bones, using tiny instruments. In this picture, Sue's jaw is being cleaned by one of the specialists.

Mending Sue's bones

The paleontologists studied each bone, and had to mend some of them. Sue's skull had been squashed by rock. It took 3,500 hours to restore it!

Scientists believe that Sue was 28 years old when she

Protecting Sue

A big trench was dug around the bones. Then it was filled with liquid plaster, which turned rock-hard and protected the bones inside.

Back to the lab

The paleontologists took the bones back to their lab in big trucks. They had to be very careful not to damage the fossils on the way.

Filling in gaps

A few of Sue's bones were missing, so paleontologists worked out what they would have looked like and made them out of plastic.

The complete Sue

Piece by piece, the bones were fitted together into the most complete skeleton of a *T. rex* ever found. A copy is now on display in Chicago, USA.

died. That was probably very old for a dinosaur.

Triceratops

Built like a giant rhinoceros with a huge head, *Triceratops* would have been an awesome sight in Cretaceous times.

Three horns

Triceratops had three big horns, as well as an impressive neck frill. Males probably fought one another for mates, crashing heads and locking horns.

The frill may have helped the dinosaur stay warm or keep cool.

Each horn was over 1 m (3 ft) long!

Triceratops used its beak-like mouth to tear its food. Its teeth – as many as 800 – could grind up tough plants.

Amazing heads

Triceratops was part of a family called Ceratopsidae, or horn-faced dinosaurs. All of the ceratopsids had impressive heads.

Defence

Triceratops lived in herds for safety and also used its horns for defence. It was strong enough to fight off big hunters, perhaps even *T. rex*.

TRICERATOPS
(tri-SERR-ah-tops)

NAME MEANING:
"Three-horned face"

PERIOD:
Cretaceous

DIET: Plants

Fossils tell us that 65 million years ago, for some reason, many dinosaurs suddenly became extinct, or died out. Nobody knows for sure why it happened.

Meteorite A disaster from space?

There is some evidence that a giant meteorite (a rock from outer space) crashed into Earth 65 million years ago and hit the Yucatán Peninsula in Mexico.

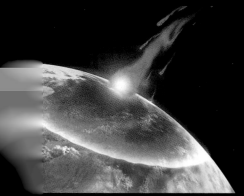

The meteorite would have travelled at 55 km per second (34 miles per second). The impact would have been huge!

The impact would have caused earthquakes, tidal waves, and volcanic eruptions around the world.

A dust cloud from the volcanoes may have killed plants and stopped sunlight from reaching Earth.

ammonites

Other extinctions

Many flying reptiles, sea reptiles, and other sea creatures (like these ammonites) also died out around the same time, 65 million years ago.

Many animals survived the meteorite and became the

A meteorite impact might have caused the weather to change over time in a way that didn't suit the large dinosaurs.

Good-bye, dinosaurs

No land creature living since has been as big, powerful, and impressive as the mighty dinosaur.

animals we know today. Why remains a mystery.

Terror birds lived in North and South America between 60 and 2 million years ago.

Terror bird
These fierce birds, now extinct, were probably related to dinosaurs and to birds alive today.

terror bird

The terror bird stood 2.5 m (8 ft) tall.

A bird's hollow bones don't fossilize well, so it's hard

Dinosaurs today

What if some dinosaurs didn't die out? Many people think that birds are related to dinosaurs.

Archaeopteryx

Archaeopteryx

Archaeopteryx, a dinosaur alive in the Jurassic period, was the earliest known bird. It had feathers, but also teeth and a bony tail.

Hoatzin

A hoatzin chick has claws on its wings that it uses to crawl up trees – maybe like *Archaeopteryx* did.

Chicken

Scientists recently compared tests of bones from a chicken and a *T. rex* and found that they are quite similar!

Cassowary

The cassowary of New Guinea and Australia has a horny crest like *Lambeosaurus* (see pages 18–19 and 53).

to work out how birds have changed over time.

History of discovery

It has been only 200 years since scientists learned that dinosaurs existed. New evidence has turned up all over the world.

1824

British scientist William Buckland announced that Plot's huge bone belonged to Megalosaurus, *a species of giant creatures, first called "dinosaurs" in 1841.*

0 CE

Large bones found in China were thought to belong to fire-breathing dragons. In fact, they were probably dinosaur bones.

1825

In England, Gideon Mantell discovered the bones of, and named, Iguanodon.

Iguanodon

1676

A huge bone, probably belonging to a dinosaur, was found by Robert Plot in England. He thought it was from a giant human.

1823

Plesiosaurus

Mary Anning discovered remains of Plesiosaurus, *a giant sea reptile, near her home in England. This proved that massive animals that are no longer alive today once existed.*

Recent technology and new fossils are giving us fresh

eagle

1938

Glen Rose Trackway was discovered in Texas, USA. These footprints of a large meat-eater and a sauropod were found by American Roland T. Bird.

2005

Studies of Archaeopteryx fossils showed that birds could be related to dinosaurs.

1990

Sue Hendrickson discovered the biggest and most complete T. rex ever found.

1923

American Roy C. Andrews led an expedition that discovered the first whole dinosaur eggs, belonging to Oviraptor, in Mongolia.

2010

For the first time ever, the exact colour of a dinosaur was discovered. Fossilized feathers of Anchiornis show that it was black and white.

information all the time. What will we discover next?

Pronunciation guide

Allosaurus
AL-oh-SORE-us

Amargasaurus
A-MARG-ah-SORE-us

Anchiornis
an-KEY-or-nis

Ankylosaurus
ang-KIE-loh-SORE-us

Apatosaurus
ah-PAT-oh-SORE-us

Archaeopteryx
ark-ee-OPT-er-ix

Argentinosaurus
AR-gent-een-oh-SORE-us

Bavarisaurus
ba-VAIR-ih-SORE-us

Camarasaurus
KAM-ar-ah-SORE-us

Ceratopsidae
serr-ah-TOP-si-day

Ceratosaurus
seh-RAT-oh-SORE-us

Coelophysis
seel-OH-fie-sis

Compsognathus
komp-sog-NATH-us

Corythosaurus
koh-RITH-oh-SORE-us

cycnodont
SIE-no-dont

Deinonychus
die-NON-i-kuss

Dimetrodon
DIE-me-troh-don

Diplodocus
DI-plod-oh-kuss

Dromaeosaurus
DROM-ee-oh-SORE-us

Edmontosaurus
ed-MON-toh-SORE-us

Europasaurus
you-ROH-pah-SORE-us

Gallimimus
gal-lee-meem-us

Gastonia
gas-TOH-nee-ah

Giganotosaurus
gi-gan-OH-toe-SORE-us

hadrosaur
HAD-row-sore

Herrerasaurus
herr-ray-rah-SORE-us

ichthyosaur
ICK-thee-oh-sore

Iguanodon
ig-WHA-noh-don

Kentrosaurus
ken-TROH-SORE-us

Lambeosaurus
lam-BEE-oh-SORE-us

Liopleurodon
LIE-oh-PLER-oh-don

Maiasaura
my-ah-SORE-ah

Megalosaurus
MEG-ah-low-SORE-us

Micropachycephalosaurus
mike-row-pak-ee-SEF-ah-loh-SORE-us

Microraptor
mike-row-RAP-tor

Oviraptor
OH-vee-RAP-tor

Pachycephalosaurus
pack-ee-SEF-al-oh-SORE-us

Parasaurolophus
pa-ra-SAW-ROL-off-us

Plesiosaurus
PLEEZ-ee-oh-SORE-us

Protoceratops
pro-toe-SERR-ah-tops

pterodactyl
terr-oh-DAC-til

pterosaur
terr-oh-sore

sauropod
SORE-oh-pod

Spinosaurus
SPINE-oh-SORE-us

Stegosaurus
STEG-oh-SORE-us

Supersaurus
SUE-per-SORE-us

Therizinosaurus
THER-ih-ZINE-oh-SORE-us

Torosaurus
tor-oh-SORE-us

Triceratops
tri-SERR-ah-tops

Troodon
TROH-oh-don

Tyrannosaurus rex
tie-RAN-oh-SORE-us rex

Velociraptor
vell-OSS-ee-RAP-tor

Glossary

coprolite
Animal poo that has been turned into a fossil.

dinosaur
An often very large reptile with four limbs and scaly or feathered skin. Dinosaurs laid eggs and lived on land. Dinosaurs died out 65 million years ago, but their descendants, birds, are alive today.

era
A very long span of time in Earth's history.

extinct
No longer in existence, having died out.

fossil
The ancient remains of an animal or plant that lived many years ago. A fossil may be animal remains, footprints, or even a plant, preserved within rock.

This Protoceratops *baby is emerging from its egg.*

frill
A large, fan-like flap of skin and bone that some dinosaurs had on their heads or necks.

herd
A group of animals that live or travel together.

ichthyosaur
A large, swimming reptile that existed at the same time as the dinosaurs.

meteorite
A piece of rock or metal from space that crashes on Earth.

paleontologist
A scientist who studies prehistoric life.

predator
An animal that hunts and eats other animals.

prey
An animal that is eaten by other animals.

pterosaur
A flying reptile with bat-like wings made of stretched skin. They lived at the same time as the dinosaurs.

reptile
A cold-blooded animal with scaly skin that lays eggs. Snakes and crocodiles are reptiles, as were dinosaurs.

sauropod
A gentle, plant-eating dinosaur, often very large, with a long neck and a long, whip-like tail.

skeleton
The complete set of bones in an animal's body.

Index

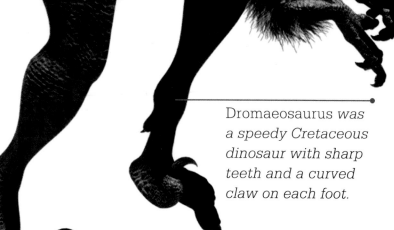

Dromaeosaurus was a speedy Cretaceous dinosaur with sharp teeth and a curved claw on each foot.

Thank you